Cats, Cats, and More Cats

for Mark, with love

First edition for the United States and Canada published
by Barron's Educational Series, Inc., 2000

First published in Great Britain in 2000 by Piccadilly Press Ltd.,
5 Castle Road, London NW1 8PR United Kingdom

All inquiries should be addressed to:
Barron's Educational Series, Inc.
250 Wireless Boulevard
Hauppauge, New York 11788
http://www.barronseduc.com

International Standard Book Number 0-7641-1589-8

Library of Congress Catalog Card No. 00-102274

The right of Dana Kubick to be recognized
as Author of this work has been asserted by her
in accordance with the Copyright, Designs, and Patents Act 1988.

Text designed by Louise Millar
Printed and bound in Belgium by Proost

*After completing her B.A., Dana Kubick
studied in the School of Visual Arts in New York.
She has illustrated over ten books, and also
designs in many different materials.
She lives in London with her partner and two cats –
one of whom, Lily, was a model in this book!*

Cats, Cats, and More Cats

Dana Kubick

BARRON'S

There are big cats.

There are small cats.

There are cats with stripes.

There are black cats . . .

. . . and spotted cats.

And some cats
are born with spots
that fade away.

There are cats that sleep in trees.

There are cats that ROAR
but never purr . . .

. . . and purring cats that
cannot roar.

One cat can purr *and* roar –
but only very softly.

Cats run fast.

Cats jump high.

Some cats like to swim.

All cats love to sleep.

There are lots of cats in the world.

But the best cat is your cat!

There are big cats.

Living in the forests of the Russian Far East, the Siberian tiger is the largest of all the cats. It can be almost 11 feet (3.3m) long, not including the tail. Male Siberian tigers can weigh up to 660 pounds (300 kgs). Siberian tigers are an endangered species. There are fewer than 450 Siberian tigers left in the wild.

And some cats are born with spots that fade away.

This is a puma with her spotted kittens; the spots fade as the kitten grows. Other plain-colored cats that have spotted kittens are the lion, jungle cat, and jaguarundi. The puma is the cat with most names—puma, cougar, mountain lion, Florida panther, and catamount. The puma's habitat ranges from arid desert to tropical forest, from Canada to South America.

Cats run fast. Cats jump high.

The African cheetah can run up to 56 mph (90 km/h) for short distances. A long streamlined body and long powerful legs help it to run so fast. Unlike other cats, its claws are always exposed, acting as running spikes.
The caracal, found in Africa and Asia, can jump 13 feet (4 m) in the air to knock birds out of the sky.

There are small cats.

The rusty-spotted cat is the cat family's smallest member. It is about half the size of a house cat, weighing less than 5 pounds (2.3 kgs) and 22 in. (55.9 cm) in overall length. Rusty-spotted cats live in Central and Southern India and Sri Lank. Rusty-spotted cats are rare, but captive kittens raised by local people are said to make good pets and are extremely affectionate.

There are cats that sleep in trees.

This is a jaguar, the largest cat of the Americas. Jaguars are good climbers, as are leopards, clouded leopards, margays, and ocelots.
Leopards, and a few other cats, carry their prey up into the branches of a tree where other animals will be una to get it.

Some cats like to swim.

This is a North American bobcat. Other wild cats that like to swim are the tiger, jaguar, leopard, serval, jaguarundi, ocelot, lynx, and, of course, the fishing cat.
The fishing cat has feet that are slightly more webbed than other cats and long claws to help it catch fish.

There are cats with stripes.

Tiger stripes are like human fingerprints—no two tigers have the same markings.
"White tigers" are actually cream-colored, with chocolate-brown stripes and ice-blue eyes.
The tiger is now one of the most endangered cats. The number of Siberian, Sumatran, South China, and Indo-Chinese tigers added together would only be a few thousand.

There are cats that ROAR but never purr . . . and purring cats that cannot roar.

Cats that roar cannot purr and purring cats can't roar. Only the "big cats" can roar: lion, tiger, leopard, and jaguar. The puma and cheetah are the only "big cats" that can't roar but do purr. This purring is an ocelot.
A lion's roar can be heard 5 miles (8 km) away.

All cats love to sleep.

All cats sleep a lot. Cats may sleep for as many as 18 hours a day.
Big cats sleep with their legs and tails stretched out, but snow leopards can sleep like a little house cat, curled up using their 3-foot (9-m) long tail wrapped around them as a nose warmer.

There are black cats and spotted cats.

The black cats that we usually call "panthers" are actually black leopards, or sometimes black jaguars, but many other cats can also be black. If you look carefully you can still see spots on a black panther.

One cat can purr *and* roar – but only very softly.

A snow leopard's throat and vocal cords are a little like those of the cats that roar and a little like those of the cats that purr. Snow leopards can almost roar but only softly, and can almost purr but not continuously.
Snow leopards can be found in the mountains of Central Asia, from Russia and Mongolia through China and Tibet to the Himalayas in India. The long thick fur of a snow leopard keeps them warm, and their large feet act like snowshoes.